EXPLORING THE SCIENCE OF NATURE

The Nature and Science of
PATTERNS

Jane Burton and Kim Taylor

Gareth Stevens Publishing
MILWAUKEE

For a free color catalog describing Gareth Stevens Publishing's list of high-quality books and multimedia programs, call 1-800-542-2595 (USA) or 1-800-461-9120 (Canada). Gareth Stevens Publishing's Fax: (414) 225-0377. See our catalog, too, on the World Wide Web: gsinc.com

Library of Congress Cataloging-in-Publication Data

Burton, Jane.
The nature and science of patterns / by Jane Burton and Kim Taylor.
p. cm. — (Exploring the science of nature)
Includes bibliographical references and index.
Summary: Describes the wide variety of patterns found throughout the plant and animal world including the petals of flowers, stripes of zebras, and scales of cones.
ISBN 0-8368-2107-6 (lib. bdg.)
1. Natural history—Juvenile literature.   2. Pattern perception—Juvenile literature.
[1. Natural history.   2. Pattern perception.]   I. Taylor, Kim.   II. Title.
III. Series: Burton, Jane. Exploring the science of nature.
QH48.B9725   1998
578.4'1—dc21   97-53093

First published in North America in 1998 by
Gareth Stevens Publishing
1555 North RiverCenter Drive, Suite 201
Milwaukee, Wisconsin 53212 USA

This U.S. edition © 1998 by Gareth Stevens, Inc. Created with original © 1998 by White Cottage Children's Books. Text and photographs © 1998 by Jane Burton and Kim Taylor. The photographs on pages 1, 6 (above, below left, and below right), 7 (all), 9 (left), 18 (right), 19 (below), and cover background are by Mark Taylor. The photograph on page 31 is by Jan Taylor. The mosaic Stegosaurus on page 29 is by Karl Mortay. Conceived, designed, and produced by White Cottage Children's Books, 29 Lancaster Park, Richmond, Surrey TW10 6AB, England. Additional end matter © 1998 by Gareth Stevens, Inc.

The rights of Jane Burton and Kim Taylor to be identified as the authors of this work have been asserted by them in accordance with the Copyright, Design and Patents Act 1988. Educational consultant, Jane Weaver; scientific adviser, Dr. Jan Taylor.

Printed in the United States of America

1 2 3 4 5 6 7 8 9 02 01 00 99 98

Contents

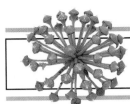

Words that appear in the glossary are printed in **boldface** type the first time they occur in the text.

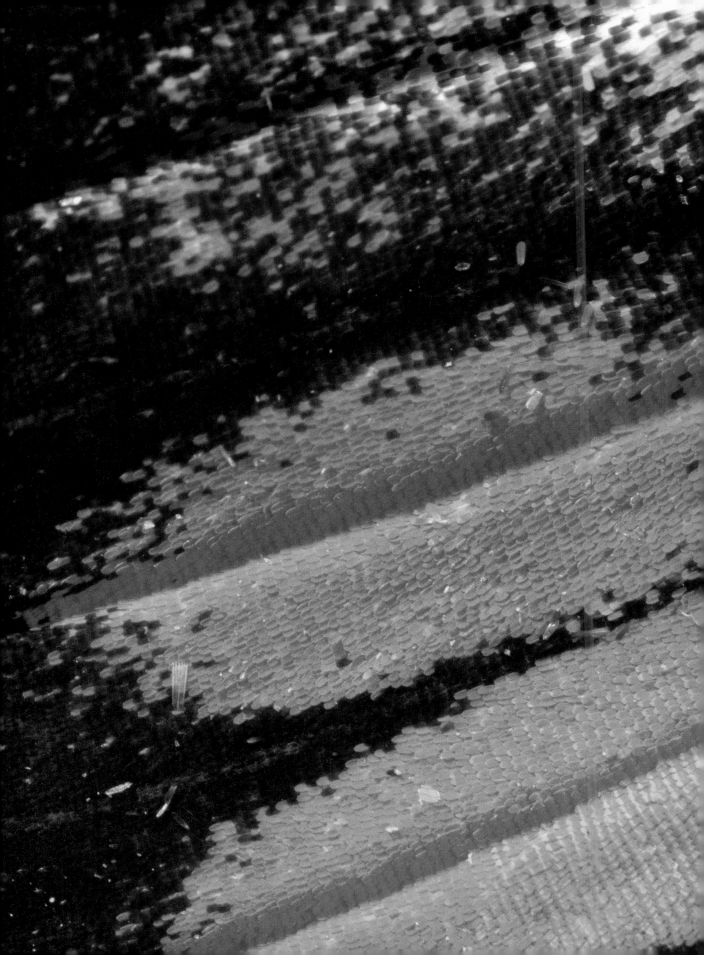

The Shape of Patterns

Opposite: The pattern on the wing of an African orange-tip butterfly is made up of thousands of scales. They are arranged in rows, like tiles on a roof.

Patterns are made of shapes that are repeated many times. The shapes, or **motifs**, in natural patterns, vary greatly. Round dots form spotted patterns. Bars of dark and light form striped patterns. The complicated shapes of leaves make their own special types of patterns. A pattern must have **repetition**. A motif that is visible in one part of the pattern must be repeated in other parts, even if it is not exactly the same shape or the same size. Without repetition, there is no pattern.

Regular patterns are formed when a motif (or several different motifs) is repeated at regular intervals. The petals of a flower may be arranged around its center regularly. Close study will show that the petals are not all identical, however. The petal motif varies. Natural patterns are not usually regular patterns. Their motifs vary in size, shape, or color. These types of natural patterns are much more pleasing to the human eye than the perfectly regular patterns made by machines.

Above: A young emperor angelfish has a pattern of stripes and spots.

Below: The adult emperor angelfish has a pattern of stripes.

Left: A leopard's spots are not actually round. They are somewhat flower shaped.

5

Infinite Variety

Much of the natural world is covered in **foliage**. Leaves come in every shape and size and make beautiful and varied patterns with the repetition of their shapes.

The leaves on any plant are usually so alike that the plant can be identified from just one of its leaves. But, in fact, no two leaves on a plant are identical. Look at several leaves on a big tree, and you will not find two that match exactly.

Leaves try to catch as much sunlight as they can, so each leaf grows away from its neighbors as much as possible to escape their shade.

Leaves form a sort of **mosaic**, which changes as the leaves move to search out the light. Such patterns are **infinitely variable** — no leaf shape and no leaf pattern are ever exactly repeated or are ever constantly the same.

Below: Some types of moss make a pattern of repeating star shapes.

Below: Wet lupine leaves make a pattern of green stars.

Left: Each thimbleberry leaf is very slightly different from the next. This creates a pattern of repeating leaf shapes.

The foliage of most plants is green, so leafy patterns are mostly green. But green in nature is rarely **monotonous** because it can change from almost blue to yellow. In autumn, the leaves of some plants change color from green to red or gold. In spring and summer, buds and flowers, then seed heads, berries, and fruits add to the pattern. Each season produces its own rich mosaic of plant colors and patterns.

Below: Fallen aspen leaves make a mosaic in shades of gold.

Below: Virginia creeper is brilliantly colored and patterned.

7

Branching Patterns

Top: A crested newt tadpole has branching gills. Its legs branch into toes.

Above: The antlers of these magnificent red deer stags show a strong branching pattern.

Right: Snow outlines the branching pattern of twigs on a tree.

Just as a plant can be identified from the shape of its leaves, each type of tree has its own pattern of branches and twigs. Branching patterns are known as **dendritic**, which means tree-like. The patterns begin with a main trunk divided into branches, which divide again and again until they become twigs. Many plants, besides trees, grow in a branching manner, and their leaves may also contain branching veins.

A few animals, or parts of animals, are also dendritic — such as branching corals, the gills of newt and frog tadpoles, and the antlers of deer.

Animals also have branching veins and nerves inside their bodies.

Sometimes a split rock will reveal a dark dendritic pattern inside it. On a much grander scale, a river system seen from the air can resemble a tree, but growing in reverse. The river starts with twig-like trickles. These join to form streams, which merge into bigger streams, and finally form a single, mighty river that flows trunk-like into the sea.

Above: Wet rot fungus growing on the floor of a damp cellar spreads in a fan-shaped, branching pattern.

Left: Little channels cut by water in sand show the same branching pattern as mighty rivers that flow to the sea. Patterns are called **fractal** when one small section looks much the same as a large area of the pattern.

Camouflage Patterns

Top: An Australian marbled gecko has a pattern of dark, wavy lines to help it blend in with its background.

Many animals need to hide from their enemies. The patterns and colors of the coats or skin of some of these animals **mimic** their surroundings. This is called **camouflage**. Camouflage patterns break up the outline of the animal, causing it to blend in with its background.

Baby animals are particularly at risk from **predators**. The coats, feathers, or skin of the babies are often patterned quite differently from their parents so they can stay hidden from enemies. The chicks of ground-nesting birds, such as pheasants and ducks, are striped in dark and light brown. Wild piglets, too, are striped, while fawns have white spots on a reddish coat. This

Right: Newly hatched game pheasants are striped (unlike the adult birds). The stripes make the chicks very difficult to see among the twigs and dead leaves of the nest.

dappled pattern mimics sunlight on the forest floor. These young animals are camouflaged so well that, when they crouch among dead leaves or other plants, they are practically invisible — as long as they remain still.

Adult animals also need camouflage. The tiger does not want to be seen — particularly when creeping up on **prey**. Its dark wavy stripes on a tawny coat are good camouflage. The stripes break up the tiger's outline and mimic sunshine and shadows in long grass or the forest.

Striped Patterns

In the animal world, a pattern of bold stripes often has a special meaning. It can give a message to other animals. Yellow-and-black stripes on the bodies of insects and other animals usually mean danger. Wasps have yellow-and-black stripes, and predators quickly learn that an insect colored in this way may sting. A yellow-and-black pattern may also be a warning to predators that an insect is distasteful or even poisonous.

The black-and-white stripes of zebras carry a different sort of message. They are not for camouflage because zebras live on the open plains of Africa, where the grass does not grow tall. They are not a danger signal, either. So why are zebras so boldly marked? A clue can be found by looking carefully at the pattern of markings on several zebras. No two zebra patterns are the same. Zebras are active at night and travel in herds, so it is important for them to know where their friends are. Their stripes allow them to recognize each other — even in the dark. The stripes may also help confuse lions. The black-and-white zebras, dashing in all directions, may dazzle and distract the lions from focusing in on and killing one. In the confusion, an entire herd of zebras may escape.

Top: A wasp's body is striped in yellow and black. These colors warn birds and other animals that wasps sting.

Opposite: The pattern of stripes on each of these common zebras is slightly different. The animals can recognize each other at a distance by the markings.

Below: Grevy's zebras are bigger than common zebras, and their stripes are much narrower.

Overlapping Patterns

Top: Pinecones are made of overlapping scales.

Fish, lizards, and snakes have scales. A single scale is a simple shape. When many scales of the same size overlap, they make a regular pattern. Small changes in the size and shape of the scales on an animal's body create intricate overlapping patterns. But a scaly skin is not just for decoration. The scales form a strong, protective layer. Because they overlap, scales can slide over each other, allowing an animal's body to bend and stretch without exposing the delicate skin underneath.

Above: Each scale of a horned viper snake has a ridge down its middle. The ridges make a pattern along the side of the snake.

Right: The bold stripes of a milk snake are made of a pattern of differently colored, overlapping scales.

14

Left: The bodies of yellow-finned barbs are protected by a layer of tough, overlapping scales.

Some plants have scales, too. The seeds of many fir trees are contained in cones formed of hard scales. The ends of the scales make an overlapping pattern on the outside of the cone. When the cone opens to release the seeds, it is sometimes possible to see that the scales are arranged on a central stalk. Leaf buds and flower buds are also often enclosed by scales, which may form diamond-shaped overlapping patterns.

Left: Cedar of Lebanon cones are made of scales. Winged seeds form inside the cones, between the scales.

Feathers overlap like scales, and they also protect delicate skin. The overlapping system of feathers not only allows birds to fly, but also traps air next to the skin. This keeps the warmth of their bodies in and the cold air out.

The colors and patterns of a bird's **plumage** are produced by patches of same-colored feathers. The overlapping patterns of the feathers themselves are often hard to see because feathers have soft edges that merge with each other. But a beautiful **scalloped** pattern develops when feathers are edged in a different shade from their main color. The pattern is all the more striking because each feather is slightly different in shape and size than its neighbors. **Progressive** changes such as these are what can make many of the patterns in nature so beautiful.

Some birds have **mottled** plumage. Their feathers have spots or bars of color instead of one plain color. Many adjoining feathers marked in a similar way produce spotted or barred patterns. Color patterns are very important to birds, allowing them to identify each other at a glance. Male birds often have strongly colored feather patterns to make them more easily seen by other males of the same species.

Somber, mottled patterns allow some birds to blend in with their surroundings.

Opposite: Overlapping feathers on the neck of a game pheasant protect its skin and trap warmth.

Above: Pale-edged feathers on the back of this two-banded courser form a clear overlapping pattern.

Below: The feathers on a sandgrouse's back have pale ends. They make a spotted pattern that helps camouflage the bird among stones.

Symmetry

Top: When viewed from above, a carline thistle flower has radial symmetry.

Above: A large tortoiseshell butterfly basks in the Sun. Its outspread wings, and patterns on them, are bilaterally symmetrical.

Right: Patches of snow on a steep mountain-side are reflected in Crater Lake in Oregon. The snow patches and their reflections make a pattern with bilateral symmetry.

Patterns can be made by shapes that are mirror images of one another. For example, each fully spread wing of a butterfly — and the pattern on it — is a mirror image of the opposite wing. The wings match each other in every respect except that the shapes and patterns are reversed. Almost all animals, outwardly at least, can be divided into two equal halves that are mirror images of each other. This **bilateral symmetry** is very important to animals that move around a lot. Without it, they would be unbalanced.

Most animals are only **symmetrical** if one side is compared with the other side. But compare head with tail, and there is no symmetry.

The tentacles or arms of some very simple animals — such as the flower-like sea anemones, corals, and starfish — **radiate** in all directions from a central point. Many flowers also have this type of symmetry, called **radial symmetry**.

18

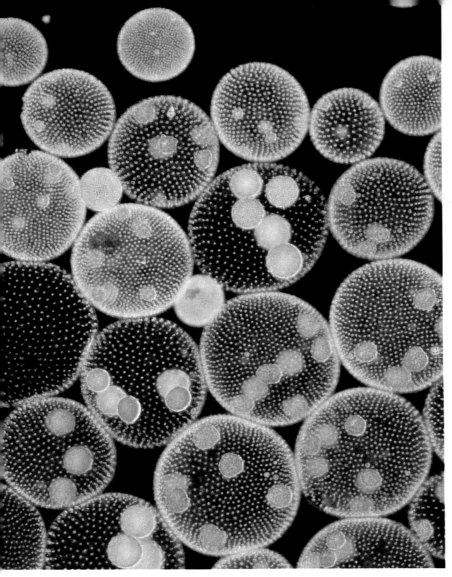

Sea anemones, flowers, and mushrooms can show radial symmetry. But they all have a top side that is different from their underside, so they are symmetrical in two **dimensions** only. Can there be symmetry in all three dimensions? The answer is *yes*. A snow crystal has radial symmetry, and its upper and lower sides match. It is symmetrical in all three dimensions.

A tiny freshwater plant, called volvox, forms beautifully symmetrical **spheres** that drift through the water, spinning slowly.

Ring Patterns

Top: The ring patterns on the hind wings of this East African emperor moth look startlingly like the eyes of an owl.

When a drop of water falls onto a still pool, ripples spread out from it in a pattern of ever-widening **concentric** rings. These ripple rings have radial symmetry. An animal's eye is also a pattern of concentric rings. The iris is a colored ring with a darker ring around its edge. A black disk, the pupil, is at the center.

The eyes of a large owl or eagle are very frightening to small birds. Ring patterns that

Right: The "eye" of the same emperor moth, viewed close-up, has a small white patch in its dark center that looks just like light reflected in a real eye.

simply mimic large eyes can be equally frightening to small birds. Some insects, such as the emperor moth, have eye-like markings on their hind wings that protect them from predators. These false eyes are hidden beneath the emperor's forewings when the moth is at rest. If a predator is nearby, the emperor flicks its forewings forward, revealing a pair of fierce staring "eyes." This may shock the predator into leaving the moth alone.

Eye-like patterns are also found on the feathers of some birds, such as peacocks and certain pheasants. The male birds with these patterns use them to impress females and communicate with other males.

Above: The pattern in an angelfish's eye consists of a series of concentric rings. Under water, a fish's eye does not have a white spot of reflected light.

Left: The eye of a little owl forms a ring pattern. A white spot of light is reflected from the surface of the eye.

Ring patterns can be found in certain types of rocks where, over millions of years, layers build up around a central core.

Stalactites and **stalagmites** form in this way. They gradually build up in caves from trickling water. When a stalactite is sliced open, a ring pattern caused by different amounts of minerals is visible.

Nodules of **agate** form in the opposite way — from the outside inward. Layers of crystals line the insides of holes in rock. The crystal layers build up gradually to form solid nodules that fill the holes.

Right: A slice through a nodule of agate shows a pattern of rings created as the nodule formed. Agate is normally blue-gray in color. This piece has been stained other colors.

A **spiral** pattern is a special type of ring pattern. Instead of the rings being separate, they are formed by a continuous curving line. An orb-web spider spins its web in a delicate spiral, hung on strands that radiate from the web's center.

The leaves or shoots of many plants grow from the stem in a spiral pattern. But the spiral is in three dimensions, with each new leaf or shoot appearing a little farther up and a little farther around the central stem. The scales on a fir cone grow from the central stem in a spiral. Snail shells also form spiral patterns. They can be flat, two-dimensional spirals or three-dimensional spirals, like twisted church spires.

Space-saving Patterns

Top: The pattern on a reticulated giraffe is made of irregular polygons. The polygons fit together because their sides can be any length and at any angle to suit the pattern.

A bubble floating on the surface of water is round. Bubbles are attracted toward each other. As soon as they touch, their shape changes. When many bubbles are drawn together to form a "raft," they become 5-, 6-, or 7-sided. This means that no space is wasted between the bubbles like there would be if they stayed round. Bubbles in a raft make a pattern of **polygons**, instead of a pattern of circles with spaces in between.

Bees and wasps use this same space-saving idea when building their nests. If the cells in which they store honey or grow their **larvae** were round, valuable space would be wasted between cells. Instead, each cell is **hexagonal** and is surrounded

Right: When round, floating bubbles join to make a raft, they squeeze together and form polygons with no spaces in between.

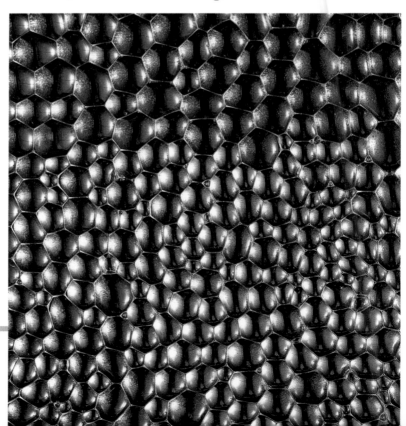

24

Left: The cells in a wasps' nest are regular hexagons that fit together neatly in rows.

Below: Wasps could build square cells instead of hexagonal ones, but their larvae and **pupae** *(pictured)* would not fit as snugly into square cells.

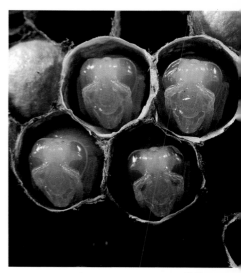

by six other cells, fitting neatly together into a honeycomb pattern. Honeycomb is one of the few regular patterns in nature.

Squares and rectangles also fit together without leaving spaces in between. But, unlike honeycomb, in which the hexagons must be regular, space-saving rectangular patterns can be made up of squares and rectangles of various sizes and shapes. Mud often dries in rectangular patterns. Dried mud sometimes looks almost as if paving stones have been laid.

The Natural Pattern

Top: The garden spider has a distinct pattern.

Below: A song thrush sings in late winter. Its repeated notes form a pattern in sound.

The first few drops of a rain shower make a pattern of spots on the dry ground. The spots do not appear to be grouped in any particular way. They form a **random** pattern. Raindrops drum steadily on a roof, without a particular beat. The raindrops are falling randomly in time as well as in space. Now listen to a bird sing or a cricket chirp. Their sounds form recognizable patterns. Music is made up of patterns in sound.

Animal behavior consists of distinct patterns. Color patterns, sound patterns, and behavioral patterns combine when colorful, glossy male birds display to females. The males perform certain patterns during courtship. These patterns are somewhat like a dance routine.

Right: A worker bee, carrying yellow pollen on its legs, rushes around, wriggling its body, while other bees watch. The worker's movements follow a distinct pattern that tells the other bees how far away and in which direction there are good flowers to visit.

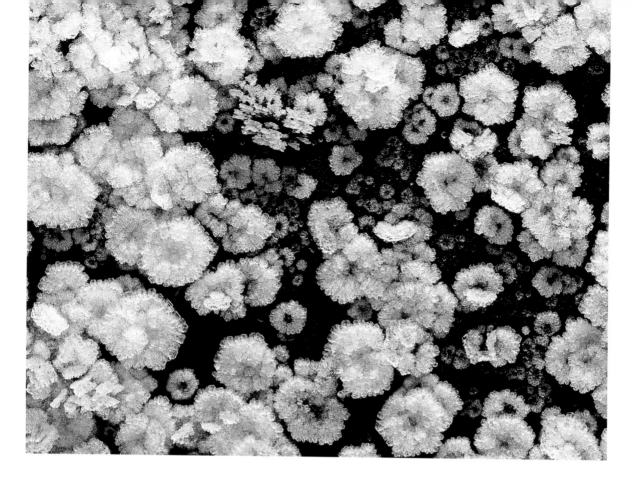

Hurricanes, volcanic eruptions, and real estate developers with bulldozers bring chaos to the natural world. Left to itself, nature can also work patiently to create patterns and order.

You can find these patterns everywhere if you look carefully. All living things make patterns. Clouds in the sky make patterns. Sand is patterned by wind and waves. Even soil and mud settle in layered patterns.

Natural patterns make the world a place of infinite variety and fascination.

Above: Frost crystals on a frozen pond form a pattern of six-sided shapes.

Below: Cumulus clouds and their shadows on the ground form patterns on a grand scale.

Activities:

Making Patterns

There are many ways to make patterns out of natural materials. Collect some handfuls of fallen leaves from under a tree. Before you start to make a pattern, try to match the leaves to see if you can find two that are identical. If the tree has simple leaves, many may look similar, but they will always vary slightly in outline or color. If the tree has more complex leaves, arrange them in a series showing how the shape changes gradually from simple to complex.

To make a pattern out of your leaves, you will need to flatten them. If the leaves are dry and curly, soak them for a while in a bowl of warm water to soften them. Then, let them drain.

Before the leaves start to dry and curl again, press them between layers of old newspapers until they are dry and flat. You will then have uniformly flat leaf shapes to work with (*below*).

Overlapping Layers

You can make a pattern by just sticking the leaves themselves onto paper using small pieces of clear tape. Or you could use the leaves as "masks" to make an overlapping pattern. To do this, you will need a sheet of thick white paper and a can of spray paint. Arrange some of the leaves on the left of

the paper (*above*). You will need to tape the leaves down lightly with double-sided tape or weigh them down with small stones to stop them from moving during painting.

When you have arranged the first row of leaves on the left of the paper, spray the entire sheet very, very lightly with paint. Use spray paint only when an adult is present, and make sure your work area is well ventilated.

While waiting for the paint to dry, select the best leaves for the next part of the design. When the first spraying is dry, tape or weigh down the next leaves on top of the first so that they overlap by half their length or more. Spray another light layer of paint over the entire paper again. Repeat these steps until you have covered the entire paper with leaves (*opposite, top*).

When the paint is thoroughly dry, gently lift off all the leaves. You have created an overlapping pattern of leaves that gets darker across the paper, from left to right (*below*). You can vary the pattern by using differently colored paints.

Mosaics

There are many other natural objects, besides leaves, with which to make patterns — for example, feathers, shells, or seeds. A beach is a great place to collect some of these items. Where the high tide has dumped masses of seaweed, you can find treasures, such as seagull feathers, shells, bones of seabirds and fish, and bits and pieces of crabs. Collect only clean and sun-dried materials.

You will need a sheet of very tough cardboard or thin plywood as a base for your mosaic and some strong glue. Arrange the objects you have collected in a pleasing design on the board. Do not use glue at this stage.

Remember that a pattern is formed by repeated shapes. Choose similar objects to form motifs, which are repeated across the board. When you are satisfied with the design, lift each object and glue it in place. When it dries, the finished design can be hung on a wall.

Mosaics do not have to be just patterns. They can also be images of many different objects, such as animals (*below*), cars, food, people, and much more.

But remember that many repetitions of the same motif make a much stronger design than just a collection of all the motifs you have found.

Glossary

agate: a very hard form of rock, made of silica.

bilateral symmetry: having two sides that are mirror images of each other.

camouflage: patterns of color on an animal (or object) making the animal or object difficult to see.

concentric: having the same center.

dappled: having a spotted pattern.

dendritic: branching like a tree.

dimensions: the directions in which the size and shape of an object are measured.

foliage: leaves, flowers, and branches.

fractal: having the same basic structure whether looked at as a whole or as a part, however small.

hexagonal: six-sided.

infinitely variable: always changing, without ever being exactly the same.

larvae: the wingless, wormlike forms of newly hatched insects.

mimic: to copy.

monotonous: a tedious sameness.

mosaic: a pattern or design made of many small pieces.

motif: the basic shape from which a pattern is built.

mottled: covered by closely spaced or overlapping spots or blotches.

nodule: a small, rounded, hard lump of a substance.

plumage: the feather covering of a bird.

polygon: a flat shape that has any number of straight sides.

predator: an animal that hunts other animals for food.

prey: an animal that is hunted by other animals for food.

progressive: changing from one form to another in small, equal amounts.

pupae: the resting stage in the development of insects before they become adults.

radial symmetry: arranged regularly around a central point.

radiate: to spread out in straight lines in all directions.

random: without any recognizable pattern.

regular pattern: a pattern arranged with the same interval of distance or time.

repetition: the repeating of a motif (or sound) several times.

scalloped: having a wavy edge.

sphere: an object that is round, like a ball.

spiral: a continuous line that curves inward or outward around a central point.

stalactite: a limestone structure hanging from the roof of a cave, formed from dripping water.

stalagmite: a limestone structure growing from the floor of a cave, formed from dripping water.

symmetrical: exactly corresponding in form on each side of a central line or around a central point.

Plants and Animals

The common names of plants and animals vary from language to language. But plants and animals also have scientific names, based on Greek or Latin words, that are the same the world over. Each plant and animal has two scientific names. The first name is called the genus. It starts with a capital letter. The second name is the species name. It starts with a small letter.

African orange-tip butterfly
(*Colotis eucharis*) — Africa 4-5

angelfish (*Pterophyllum scalare*) —
Amazon 21

cedar of Lebanon (*Cedrus libani*) —
Middle East, planted elsewhere 15

common zebra (*Equus burchelli*) — Africa
12-13

death's head hawkmoth (*Acherontia atropos*) — worldwide 11

East African emperor moth (*Gynasa maja*)
— Africa 20

emperor angelfish (*Pomacanthus imperator*) — tropical seas 5

game pheasant (*Phasianus colchicus*) —
Asia, introduced elsewhere 10, 16-17

grevy's zebra (*Equus grevyi*) — Ethiopia,
Somalia, Kenya 13

honeybee (*Apis mellifera*) — worldwide 26

leopard (*Panthera pardus*) — Africa, Asia 5

little owl (*Athene noctua*) — Europe 21

milk snake (*Lampropeltis triangulum*) —
northwestern United States 14

namaqua sandgrouse (*Pterocles namaqua*)
— southwestern Africa 17

ponderosa pine (*Pinus ponderosa*) —
North America 6

red deer (*Cervus elaphus*) — northern
Europe 8

reticulated giraffe (*Giraffa camelopardalis*)
— eastern Africa 24

song thrush (*Turdus philomelos*) —
Europe 26

thimbleberry (*Rubus parviflorus*) —
North America 7

tiger (*Panthera tigris*) — Asia 11

two-banded courser (*Hemmerodromus africanus*) — Africa 17

wet rot fungus (*Fibroporea vaillantii*) —
worldwide 9

yellow-finned barb (*Barbus species*) —
southeastern Asia 15

Books to Read

Animal Survival (series). Michel Barré
(Gareth Stevens)
Bees: Busy Honeymakers. Secrets of the Animal World (series). Eulalia García
(Gareth Stevens)
Catch Me If You Can! Nature Close-ups (series). Densey Clyne (Gareth Stevens)

Life in the Forest. Eileen Curran (Troll)
Pond Water Zoo. Peter Loewer (Atheneum)
Welcome to the World of Animals (series).
Diane Swanson (Gareth Stevens)
Woodlands. Victor Mitchell (Lion USA)
Young Naturalist Field Guides (series).
(Gareth Stevens)

Videos and Web Sites

Videos

The Art of Nature. (Camera One)
Art of the Wild. (Foundation for Global Community)
Design and Nature. (International Film Bureau)
Discovering Natural Patterns. (AIMS)
Nature's Camouflage. (AIMS)

Web Sites

www.arabianwildlife.com/vol2.1/cama.htm
www.rytter.com/Brittany's/Brittany.html
www.vol.it/MIRROR2/EN/CAVE/staltite.html
www.cc.gatech.edu/gvu/multimedia/nsfmmedia/graphics/elabor/math/mathfaq_polys.html

Some web sites stay current longer than others. For further web sites, use your search engines to locate the following topics: *camouflage*, *hexagons*, *polygons*, *stalactites*, and *stalagmites*.

Index